# GOOD MORNING, DEAR FATHER

## Robert Coyle

PRESS

www.xulonpress.com

It's Your Book, Dear Father.

Use It As You Will.

# CONTENTS

# INTRODUCTION

Why is a book written? Why does one write a book? Some write a book so that someone will read it. The Bible was written, but not everyone will read it. Some write a book to motivate others. Some write to inspire. Some write to teach. Some write to chronicle events. Some write to express love. Some write to impart mystery. Some write to entertain. Some write to give directions. Some write to predict future events. All of these and many more are found in the writings of The Holy Scriptures, and yet the major motive of the Scriptures is to set the stage for the pre-planned arrival of Jesus Christ, The

Son of God, and portray His life with the express purpose of reconciling man to The Almighty God.

As history relates, we all stray away from our Creator. Some of us never return. I am one of the lucky ones who returned from so far and so my "far away" made the return so much more exciting. I had distanced myself from God for fifteen plus years.

Two Scriptures captured my attention as I saw my circumstances and realized that we are the "theys" in Scripture.

> Yet The Lord still waits for you to come to Him so He can show you His love; He will conquer you to bless you, just as He said. For the Lord is faithful to this promise. Blessed are all those who wait for Him to help them (Isaiah 30:18).

---

But I will not give up – I will plead for you to return to me, and will keep on pleading;

yes, even with your children's children in the years to come (Jeremiah 2:9).

In writing this book, I covet your attention so that my experiences and joys may encourage you to have a life-long, daily encounter with God. Like David, I must tell you what He did for me (See Psalm 66:16).

There has been a negligence in writing this book because of so many expanded thoughts that need to be told. It is like the Apostle John who happily ends his gospel (John 21:25) by speaking of there being so much to tell about Jesus that it would fill more books than this world could ever hold? Was John's closing remark an indication of relief and happiness because he had finished his gospel or was it John's way of saying that Jesus keeps adding experiences to our lives each day and therefore neither is our story

and relationship with The Blessed Savior ever over?

# CHAPTER 1

# GENERAL PIECES

—⁓—

P<u>rayer</u>: Heavenly Father, assemble the pieces as You see fit.

This book, "Good Morning, Dear Father" is my attempt to chronicle the exhilarating experiences and discernments over the past four years as the Quiet Time has been a part of my daily life. I sensed my mission to write this book to document the many benefits of the Quiet Time to one's individual spiritual growth. The Quiet Time if encouraged among a total church's congregation could make the church's corporate worship a power house of Spirit filled congregants. This book is about me – The King and I. It is written in hopes that it will help you to write a book about you – The King and you.

<u>Prayer</u>: Heavenly Father, may the quiet time with You be the finest moments we spend each day, and please use us wherever we are in our spiritual journey to glorify You.

<u>Untold Secrets</u>

The Quiet Time – I had never heard of it before the year, 2004. I had grown up in the church (Presbyterian). Never do I recall hearing anything about the Quiet Time (from now on referred to as the QT.) Was it something that only a few participated in? Was it something potentially so powerful that the spiritual leaders of the church kept it as a secret among themselves? Was it a neglected (forgotten practice) opportunity for communion with God that was experienced by some and yet not discussed and shared among those who participated?

In August, 2004, my daughter, Cheryl, gave me a book titled, *My Utmost for His Highest* (Oswald Chambers) that provided a one page, daily diet of devotional readings. Also, in my volunteer assignments at Covenant Presbyterian Church in San Antonio, Texas, I had come across a video-based program, *Praying To Make A Difference, A Practical Guide For A Powerful Prayer Life* by Jim and Kaye Johns. That course was my initial introduction to the QT as I had the pleasure of facilitating its use among some of the congregation. In the meantime, I had started praying (new to me) and reading the Scriptures (new to me). I would check off each book of The Bible as I finished it. In spite of using The Living Bible (paraphrase version), I was certainly a long way from understanding what I read. The same was true of Chambers' book which also was a part of my daily reading regimen.

## Enthused and Infused

Prayer seemed to be the major component of the QT. God gave me an insatiable appetite to know more about prayer. Through the last five years I read twenty-five plus books on prayer and God wonderfully infused and enthused me with His messages about prayer.

God began showering me with numerous synchronistic, curious happenings. I had read that it would be good to pray for a Divine Appointment each day. I can promise you that if you pray that prayer, He will answer it. Someone or some incident will cross your path in a spiritual way. You may not recognize it until you sharpen your awareness to be alert to it. At times you will pray that prayer and then come to the end of the day and think that no Divine Appointment (Encounter) has occurred, and then upon reflecting on your day, it will be revealed to you what the appointment was.

You will begin to realize that God is a step-by-step person. God began preparing me in the area of prayer. I had read of people's dreams and visions in the Scriptures as well as in current day times. Frankly,

I wasn't sure what I would do with a vision or a "spiritual" dream if I had one. Instead, my most memorable message came in what I call Realtime. When it happened to me, I came home and wrote down what happened. Below is a record of that happening.

On March 5, 2005, I had prayed in the early morning for God to give me an affirming message in some way that a certain curriculum program was according to His Will. I even used the word, "Vision" in my prayer. While driving back home from shopping, I was slowing down to stop at a red light. I was in the left lane. Suddenly a small white pickup truck moved from the right lane and carelessly pulled in front of me. The small truck had a camper on it. Affixed to the cover of the truck was the manufacturer's name, VISION. As my eyes looked down to the license plate frame, the words, "Life Is Fragile, Handle With Prayer" surrounded the license.

I was hooked. I wanted to tell. Who would listen? Would they believe me or think I had made it up? That was then. I am different now than I was then. The QT has changed me, or perhaps I should say the QT has been the daily event that allows an increasing intimacy with God, my Savior, Jesus Christ, and The Holy Spirit. That intimacy gradually eliminates any surprise circumstances, happenings, or events that become realizations of the manifest presence of The Holy Spirit.

So many other happenings have been my stimulus to be alert to His Presence. I can promise you that the same thing will happen to you if you give yourself to the daily QT. As I said, for 15 years I had not given

God the time of day or night although earlier days had

not brought me up that way.

> Then the people of Israel turned away from
> the Lord again and worshiped the heathen
> gods, Baal, Ashtaroth, and the gods of Syria,
> Sidon, Moab, Ammon and Philistia. Not only
> that, but they no longer worshipped Jehovah
> at all (Judges 10:6).

Bad people – bad me. I had replicated the

people of Israel. There was nothing to be proud of.

Controlled by my own desires and although not

consciously wanting my own way, I had little interest

in The Way.

> Dear brothers, I have been talking to you
> as though you were still just babies in the
> Christian life, who are not following the Lord,
> but your own desires. I cannot talk to you as I
> would to healthy Christians, who are filled
> with the Spirit. I have had to feed you with
> milk and not solid food, because you couldn't
> digest anything stronger. And even now you
> still have to be fed on milk. For you are still

only baby Christians, controlled by your own desires, not God's (1 Corinthians 3:1-3).

<u>Prayer</u>: Good morning, Dear Father. It is so exciting to receive your creative messages that beyond question are You communicating with me. Help me to continue being alert to the spiritual among the secular parts of my life. Encourage and guide others to want to sense spiritual manifestations in their lives. And Dear Lord, let me and others grow up and not be sucklings. In His Precious Name. Amen!

# CHAPTER 2

# TIME AND PLACE

～～

Good Morning, Dear Father.

I remember wanting to "have" a QT. I remember being a little embarrassed for others in my household to know that I was hiding behind closed doors or to see me with the Bible out. What do I have to do? What does God do? Are there time restrictions or expectations? How many pages of Scripture do I have to read each morning? Do I pray? Are their certain prayer postures that I must abide by? Should I use a devotional book of some kind? How does one "meditate" on the Holy Scriptures read? Do I really have to shut the door when I go into my room for the QT? What benefits will I gain by committing time to the QT? I realized later that early on I had asked many of the same questions that Philip Yancey had asked in his book, *Prayer, Does It Make A Difference.*

While our natural inclination would be to want to know the answers to the above questions and probably many others, we can take comfort in Bob Sorge's encouragement (Secrets *Of The Secret Place.* 119).

> "God wants to lead you into a hidden place in Him where you develop your own unique connection with Him, and you come to know Him totally independent of everyone else. He wants you to develop your own secret history of communing with Him and knowing Him. No man is to teach you how to find this knowing relationship with God; The Holy Spirit Himself will be your teacher. All you must do is shut the door."

Bob Sorge beautifully writes of a secret place that all can know – a secret that does not have to be kept. He identifies the secret as the secret place. So be of good cheer. You will have the finest teacher and there is no tuition, fees, or dormitory expenses – just your time devotion to the QT – not clock time but heart time. Jim and Kaye Johns (*Praying To Make A Difference*) caution that prayers that make a difference are the ones that have been fostered by giving God undivided time and attention – meaning that our goal must be to live in spiritual intimacy with God. In their book, *Experiencing Prayer With Jesus, The Power of His Presence and Example*, Henry and Norman Blackaby ask the question, "Are you staying long enough in the Father's presence to allow Him to reveal to you His ways, truths, understanding and agenda?" (P 45) I think the answer is that God honors all time that we seek to be in His presence. I believe He delights when we crave His Word so much that we can't put The Book down. I am impressed that our Heavenly Father is patient with us regardless of how much time we spend with Him. I think I have heard Him say, "Start – stay as long as you can – come back tomorrow – don't ever stop coming – you will find Me. I will not hide from you." Eddie Smith (*How To Be Heard In Heaven*) writes, "To expect results in prayer without developing a relationship with God is ludicrous. To develop a relationship with God without expecting results, insults God. (P 58).

"But whenever you pray, go into your room and shut the door and pray to your Father who is in secret; and your Father who sees in secret will reward you"

(NRSV, Matthew 6:6). Was this meant to imply that we cannot pray anywhere other than in the privacy of our room shut off from all others behind the closed door? What do you think? "Isaac went into the field (Genesis 24:63); Christ to a mountain; Peter to a housetop. The issue is retirement to privacy to avoid distraction, allow for greater freedom in what we tell God, and avoidance of pride by being observed by others while we are speaking to God." (Matthew Henry, *Commentary On The Whole Bible, Complete and Unabridged*, Page 1637).

I resolved that I would pray. I would ask for things. I would believe that God would hear me and answer me. Did I really believe that? I did not realize that praying with doubt became an insult to God. Neither did I realize that my faith and trust would have to grow in order to have an effective prayer life.

> Sweet hour of prayer, sweet hour of prayer,
> That calls me from a world of care
> And bids me at my Father's throne
> Make all my wants and wishes known.

(Text: William W. Walford, 1772-1850; Music: William Bradbury, 1816-1868)

You mean a whole hour? God answered that question very quickly. "You can have a longer appointment if you want it. It is a privilege that I give you. We need to get to know each other better. I know everything about you, but there is much that you need to know about Me." The wonder of prayer is that God requests the audience. He invites us. We are on different levels of intimacy with God, and I was near the bottom level. Early on, results of prayer were doubtful or should I say more kindly, I was suspicious that I would probably not see their answer. Gradually as my intimacy progressed in the QT, I discerned His responses to prayer, and that began to magnify my trust in Him. Little did I understand at the beginning that there were at least four facets that had to become prerequisite traits in order for prayer to be honoring and contributing to God's glory. I believe these traits will be a life-long continuing spiritual pursuit and development in each of us. These four facets of prayer are the four that The Holy Spirit has impressed on me. They are BELIEVE, FAITH, OBEDIENCE, AND SURRENDER. I do not intend to describe all the ramifications of these four. Like Bob Sorge, I know that the Lord will work that out with each individual in His own time. I do know that each facet allows for "prayer prompts" during the QT, and I know that personally, the QT constantly contributes to the "growth" of these facets in one's life. Rather than seek to enhance an individual facet until there is a greater "mastery", just zero in on all four each day. The Holy Spirit is goal-centered in our behalf.

Prayer: Heavenly Father, I want to spend time with You. You have given me the knowing invitation of a lifetime.

> And when you draw close to God, God will draw close to you.
>
> (James 4:8)

Let each of us gratefully send response to His RSVP request as we acknowledge His invitation.

I had never thought about the reality that I had the distinct privilege of determining the level of relationship with God, nor had it dawned on me that if

I tried to draw close to God, He would draw near to me. Was God allowing me to have the initial control of contact? I think so. God never begs us to do anything.

Past Time

Had I waited too long to discover (be led to) the QT? Had I wasted too many years? For all of us, the latter years (who knows how many) can be by far the most fruitful and satisfying season of our lives. The Holy Scriptures provide more than ample GPS directions for the road trip of life.

Open my eyes to see wonderful things in your Word. I am but a pilgrim here on earth: how I need a map – and your commands are my chart and guide (Psalm 119:18-19).

Your words are a flashlight to light the path ahead of me, and keep me from stumbling (Psalm 119:105).

Beginning the QT can be the most productive part of your spiritual journey. Beginning the QT can always be productive regardless of when you begin it. Our Heavenly Father is always available, and the invitation to communion (talk with Him) is always extended. Wasted years? Yes, many. When God brings back the past to our attention, we realize that there have been shut doors, "which we have shut – doors which had no need to be shut" (Oswald Chambers, *My Utmost For His Highest*, April 3). These shut doors of our memories may bring self rebuke and sorrow, but they also become wonderful lessons of growth for our future.

Future Time

One of the joys of the QT is that it gives us discerned truths beyond all imagination. These discerned truths become encouraging to us as we realize The Holy Spirit's guidance and revelation of Truth. Bob Sorge (*Secrets of the Secret Place*. 28) speaks of stepping into God's time zone and not allowing pressing matters to become hindrances. So is the QT God's time or my time? It is His – my – Ours.

Prayer: Heavenly Father, help me to know when to speak and when to be quiet during the QT. Help me to learn how to "realize" You. Let my love for the QT never end. In His Precious Name and for His Namesake, Amen.

# CHAPTER 3

# PRAYER

P rayer is the main activity in the QT. This presents an immediate dilemma. I suspect that the main hindrance to QT practice is prayer. I have had the distinct joy of discovering that the more you pray, the more you want to pray. That is why I am so sold on the QT. God led me to read over two dozen books on prayer. That doesn't sound like many, but it was for me because I didn't pray very often and I certainly didn't read about prayer.

## A Missing Link

A link means something is either connected or disconnected. J. Vernon McGee *(I. Vernon McGee On Prayer And Living In The Father's Will. vii)* writes, "According to my humble judgment, the greatest need of the present day church is prayer. Prayer should be the vital breath of the church but right now it is gasping for air." And then he writes, "Most of our trouble and our problems can be traced back to the poverty of our prayer life." What an indictment on the very activity that God has sanctioned and made possible as a gift bought by the atonement act of His very own son!

## Satan's Schemes

Among Satan's greatest triumphs is his seemingly easy way of convincing God's people that praying is hard work and sort of useless since prayers aren't answered very often. Both of those are true. Prayer is hard work. As J. Vernon McGee states, "Real prayer requires laborious effort. It requires arduous work, eternal endurance, and plenty of pain. Real prayer is an exercise of the soul that develops spiritual muscles." (McGee, 36). Another Satanic scheme is convincing us that prayer is useless. This is based not on what God does or does not do, but it is based on what we do or don't do. It is true that unanswered prayer is dry and dead. There is not much encouragement to pray when we don't get to see the result of our prayers. "Unanswered" prayers breed unbelief and that progresses to the prayer poverty previously mentioned by McGee. God looks forward to answering our prayers because it glorifies Himself, that is if we remember to thank Him for responding and share with others what He has done.

For those (most of us) who might succumb to the perceived unanswered prayer, Philip Yancey *(Prayer, Does It Make A Difference, 2006)* removes this agony over the issue of unanswered prayer by advising that we focus our attention on companionship rather than petition.

Eddie and Alice Smith *(The Advocates, How To Plead The Case Of Others In Prayer, 2001)* remind us of another Satanic scheme that contributes to reduced praying. That is our impatience for an answer. We want the NOW response if not sooner, and when we don't get the quick response, doubt creeps in and we begin wondering if prayer works.

The Scriptures are one big prayer book. They are full of God's promises that He invites us to consider when we pray. He invites prayer and intends to respond. We get so excited about asking for whatever we will that we forget the unhidden pre-requisites for successful praying. It is these four pre-requisites that Satan capitalizes on hiding from us. It is these four pre-requisites that God wants to help us learn. As mentioned earlier, they are: BELIEVE, FAITH, OBEDIENCE, SURRENDER. The four pre-requisites seem to be God's expectations for successful prayer. Eddie Smith *(How To Be Heard In Heaven. 10-11)* puts it in perspective as he recalls the cell phone commercial long past that posed the question, "Can you hear me now?" He further writes that, "we shouldn't forget that it's the person not the prayer, that God hears. He doesn't answer prayer. God answers praying people. So in your quest to be heard, become a person God listens to." *(How To Be Heard In Heaven. 11)* Let it be you and me that God listens to.

<u>Prayer</u>: Heavenly Father, Let it be that I am one who believes in You as The Provider, The Comforter, The One I want to surrender myself to and live as one with You. Amen. Let our strive for total surrender be characterized as Oswald Chambers *(My Utmost For His Highest.* July 13) describes it.

> "Your priorities must be God first, God second, and God third, until your life is continually face to face with God and no one else is taken into account whatsoever."

John Maxwell *(Partners In Prayer.* 14) addresses the issue, Why Believers Don't Pray. He states the factual revelation that many Christians spend as little time communicating with God as nonbelievers and asks the questions, "Why is that?" He believes that people don't spend much time praying because they have the wrong attitude toward prayer. "Is prayer too mechanical? Do they run out of things to say after the first five minutes? Do they feel guilty for not having a better prayer life?" Maxwell advises us not to let the mechanics of prayer get in the way of loving God. Maxwell suggests that we should let God love us – that God is always waiting to tell us He loves us – every minute of every day, because we, "have value thanks to Jesus Christ."

Clumsy and Fear Defeated

When God encourages us to start and stick with our prayer life, I believe He lets us know ahead of time that we will be clumsy at first. Sandy Sturch describes many of us in her booklet, *Bible For the Bewildered and Prayer for the Tongue-Tied*. We are particularly attacked by the evil one when we have to pray in public like at a meeting or asking the "blessing" before a meal if that is not our custom. This fear of praying can be defeated by our daily QT. We "get better" at it and God is patient with us. Progression in our prayer life grows more mature to the extent that ultimately we become spontaneous in speaking up as we petition and seek to intercede in behalf of others.

I see this in my small group Bible study each week as we begin and as we end. The breakfast tacos need to be blessed and then prayer requests are invited at the end. You can feel the unstated discomfort in the room as silence begins to surface. Will I be asked to pray? This should not be but it is the reality of far too many of God's people who may not be growing in this element of communion conversation called prayer. At times I wonder if the fear of prayer is based on one's feeling of inadequacy or the fear that the devil will fight our growing relationship with God. It is probably both depending on the individual. Joyce Meyer *(Enjoying Everyday Life, Straight From The Heart)* admits that the devil will fight a prayerful lifestyle, but she also says that we should disregard this fear because the Bible assures us of the Lord's protection. She advises, "Make the devil mad and just be happy anyway."

## Improved Regimen

Some of us are hesitant about praying for fear we don't know the correct way. Writers have surveyed all the prayers written in the Scriptures and while even the posture of prayer (standing, kneeling, sitting, etc.) is analyzed, there is good evidence that there is no wrong way to pray for starters. As we continue our communion with God in the QT, we sense a feeling of refinement in our prayers. A part of this is stimulated as we become more familiar with God's Word. Another refinement to our prayer life is enhanced by the teaching and our sensing the presence of The Holy Spirit. J. Vernon McGee (*J. Vernon McGee On*

*Prayer.* 50) writes that, "True prayer is possible only through the power of The Holy Spirit." This praying in The Holy Spirit isn't easy to understand. The book of Romans gives us some insight:

And in the same way – by our faith – The Holy Spirit helps us with our daily problems and in our praying. For we don't even know what we should pray for, nor how to pray as we should; but The Holy Spirit prays for us with such feeling that it cannot be expressed in words (Romans 8:26-28).

There will be many times when we won't know what to pray for. McGee says that happens because we do not have heaven's perspective. He further states in a cautionary way: "Prayer is not for us to get God into line with our little will, but to get us into line with His Will" (McGee 52). The longer we visit the QT, the more keenly alert we are to The Holy Spirit and His wise counsel that refines our prayers.

"Prayer is like the Word of God – we don't read enough today for the entire week. We must have daily bread or manna. Likewise, we must go to the secret place daily, and when we do, we can spend the night there. Tomorrow, however, we must go again." (Dutch Sheets, *Intercessory Prayer, How God Can Use Your Prayers To Move Heaven and Earth.* 82).

Musical Prayer Prompts

Favorite hymns can become prayer prompts for our progressive communion with our God, our Savior, and The Holy Spirit. Let us look at a few of my favorites from my church hymnal (Tom Fettke, *The Hymnal For Worship and Celebration*). Use the praise expressed in the hymn during your QT or pray

the words of the hymn in your own words.

<u>Spirit Of The Living God</u> (Daniel Iverson, 1935, Moody Press; See Fettke #247)

> Spirit of The Living God, fall fresh on me.
> Melt me, mold me, fill me, use me.

<u>Prayer</u>: Heavenly Father, let me be more conformed

to Your Way and not my way. Start all over with me

in my rebirthing time and prepare me with a new,

Christ-centered personality that will be useful to

Your purposes. In His Precious Name, Amen.

<u>Breathe On Me</u>
<u>Breath Of God</u>        (Text: Edwin Hatch, 1835-
                 1889; Music: Robert
                 Jackson 1842-1914; See
                 Fettke #259)
Breathe on me, Breath of God.
Fill me with life anew
That I may love what Thou dost love

And do what Thou wouldst do.
Breathe on me Breath of God,
Until my heart is pure,
Until my will is one with Thine.

<u>Prayer</u>: Good Morning, Dear Father. I want The Holy
Spirit to not only reside in me but to have control of
me. May my life be so completely surrendered to the
Lordship of Christ that I may represent and exalt Him
in a worthy manner. In His Precious Name, Amen.

<u>Welcome, Welcome</u>    (Text: Lelia N. Morris;
            Music: David Read;
            Arrangement: Kurt
            Kaiser; Word Music,
            1986; See Fettke #260)
Welcome, welcome, welcome, welcome!
Holy Ghost
We welcome Thee. Come in power and fill
this temple
Holy Ghost, we welcome Thee.

<u>Prayer</u>: Good Morning, Dear Father. Thank you for
answering Jesus' call to send The Holy Spirit. Let
me become the most beautiful temple that extols

Your Love so that The Holy Spirit is not only a welcome guest but a permanent boarder. In His Precious Name, Amen.


New Technology

I am still in the early stages of computer literacy, except I should say, illiteracy, and it is that illiteracy that continues to cause me to lose things that I input on the keyboard. Up until May, 2009, I had resisted the "new" technology that was already so very old since its beginning. The depression and distur-bances accompanying my entry into the computer world was often overpowering until I prayed that God would not let the computer consume my thoughts and take my focus off Jesus Christ. He honored that prayer, and I can now say that I know where the <u>Power</u> button is, and I can turn it on. It is then <u>Loaded</u> with all kinds of things, but primarily, it is loaded with security. I already had access to the "power button". I had heard that was a prime consideration. I just hadn't tried this technology available to me by Jesus' atoning act. I didn't have to purchase any extra security for communicating and surfing on God's Internet.

One of my friends and some of my family had "signed up" for Facebook. I don't even know what it is except that I had heard talk of people asking other people, "Will you be my friend?" I went to the internet to read about this and found another action word commonly used – "You can <u>friend</u> people." I briefly read about an increasing number of social messaging centers. One is called "Twitter" and is defined as a <u>free</u> (no charge) social messaging (whatever social messaging means) utility (process) of quick (limit your wordiness), frequent (daily) answer to one simple question: What are you doing?

Will Facebook and other similar avenues be an alternative to expressed needs, greetings, praises, concerns for others, and on and on? The hymn, What A Friend We Have In Jesus (Text: Joseph Scriven, 1819-1886; Music: Charles C. Converse, 1832-1918; See Fettke #435) seems to parallel some of the elements of the Facebook.

### <u>What A Friend We Have In Jesus</u>

What a Friend we have in Jesus,
All our sins and griefs to bear!
What a privilege to carry
Everything to God in prayer!
Can we find a friend so faithful
Who will all our sorrows share?

Do thy friends despise, forsake thee?
Take it to the Lord in prayer.

Jesus, will You be my friend? What does it cost?
Can we have a good time (social) talking? Is prayer
the right way, and do I have to be brief? I hope you
don't mind, but I really enjoy talking to You daily.
Can I help? Lord, God, I want to be addicted to the
Faith Book and not the Facebook.

Let me promise you that God's Internet is never
old or obsolete. It is always new. His conversations
with us and our conversations with Him never get
outdated even though we talk with Him daily. You
will never have to replace your program. You may
have to renew certain commitments. You will never
worry about prayer procedures to connect. You will
never have to re-enter the correct address in order to

connect. And you will never be kept waiting or told to, "Try again later."

Jim and Kaye Johns *(Praying To Make A Difference.* 14) warmly divulge a major truth: Consistent time spent with God "leads to prayer that becomes two-way communication. God becomes real. No one can tell us what that is like. We have to experience Him for ourselves."

# CHAPTER 4

# GOD'S WORD

—◦◦◦—

I had heard that the QT was not a monologue time for me to do all the talking (praying). It was "supposed" to be a dialogue time when I listed to God at least part of the time. But was I deaf? Would God speak to me in a different language (in different tongues, whatever that meant)? Could I learn to be a better listener to the most important person in my life? Would I need to go on a "talking fast"? "Help me, Lord to keep my mouth shut and my lips sealed" (Psalm 141:3). I talk too much.

A Scheme of Discouragement

The Bible (which is the real one?) was pretty long. I had never read it all. Extracts had been used to teach occasional lessons in the past, but deep down I had experienced the planted idea of the evil one – "you can't understand the Bible. It's too complicated." The dilemma was that I wanted to listen to God talking to me and I suspected that He certainly might use the Scriptures as a letter to me. Even so, I couldn't help but wonder why God "made" the Bible so hard to understand if He wanted us to hear from Him.

I ultimately understood that He had His motives. For one thing, He wants us to discover for ourselves, as The Holy Spirit guides us, that we can understand more and more as we spend more time with Him. An unknown writer of the Book of

Hebrews sought to encourage his readers not to stall

in their understanding of God's Word. The writer

says that we can't stay as a baby-Christian. If so,

we will never be able to eat solid spiritual food and

understand deeper meanings of God's Word (See

Hebrews 5:12-14).

I had several Bibles at home. Some had been

given as gifts. Some were purchased. Which was

"The Bible"? Most were on a shelf in a closet. Far

too long a period had passed in my life, and I had

not given God's Word the time of day or the time of

night. I did take The Living Bible (The Way 1971)

out of the closet. It was a paraphrase "model" which

I thought would be easier to understand. After all, the

back page, 1117, had an endorsement by the great

evangelist, Billy Graham.

> "In this book I have read the age-abiding
> truths of the Scriptures with renewed interest
> and inspiration as though coming direct to
> me from God. This paraphrase communicates
> the message of Christ to our generation. Your
> reading it will give you a new understanding
> of the Scriptures."

I was no Billy Graham, but as he said, "your

reading it will give you a new understanding of

the Scriptures." That is what I wanted – a new

understanding.

Like me, you might wonder. How can I under-

stand The Bible? You can't unless you have The

Holy Spirit reading it with you and helping you to

interpret. I began asking each morning in my QT

prayer that I would receive the messages that God

wanted me to receive.

## Passionate Pursuit

With dedicated pursuit and powerful, misplaced passion, I began reading through "the" Bible, starting on page one. I had read of plans and suggestions about how to "go through" the Bible in a year. The formulas seemed complicated and I mistakenly thought that the Bible was sequential in the order that the books were assembled and bound. Admittedly, I, like many others, got bogged down in some things like genealogy of begats, but I was determined. I proudly encouraged myself by marking when (date) I started and when I finished a certain book. I "began" on April 13, 2004 and "finished" on October 25, 2004. Ah, not in a year, but in six months! This was a matter of pride. No big deal. There was no celebration at the end. As I look back now, it was just the beginning that has no end. But at that moment, the misplaced passion was motivated by the thought, "I did it." I, I, I was more persevering than I thought. It wasn't the kind of perseverance called for though.


Personally Picked

God had another secret for me to discover and that was that He would reveal His messages to me in what I read in such a manner that they seemed to match with my present degree of spiritual maturity. The Word never gets old. It has the same truths, but those truths are discerned in accordance with how intimate our relationship is with God. He will individually tailor His Word to your present ability to understand. Many times, God does the picking of what to read and then let's you think you did the picking. The daily QT scripture reading will become an individualized, programmed learning experience. God will lead you to where He wants you to read.

You will begin to realize that the Bible is not just the historical story of people long gone. It is our story as well. It is the story of God's perfect plan of communion and relationship with us. It is filled with words and thoughts about trust, obedience, mercy, disobedience, redemption, remnants, love, testing, sacrifice, justice, righteousness, provision, forgiveness, reverence, don't be afraid, and many others. Most importantly, spending daily time in The Word allows us to see Jesus Christ in all of the Bible.

My impression and I believe it will be yours as well, is the message that The Loving God clearly says to us as we read His Holy Word, "I want your attention." We in turn are given the right through Jesus to say, "I want Your attention too". And then we hear the promising response, "You've got it.".

> Your words were found, and I ate them, and Your Word was to me a joy and rejoicing of my heart (Jeremiah 15:16 NKJV).

The hymn, Guide Me, O Thou Great Jehovah (William Williams 1717-1791. See Fettke #51) speaks of the march of the Israelites from Egypt to Canaan and the 40 years of daily provision by God.

> Guide me, O Thou Great Jehovah, pilgrim through this barren land; I am weak, but Thou art mighty – hold me with Thy powerful hand: Bread of Heaven, Bread of Heaven, feed me till I want no more.

The physical manna was their daily food provision, and they prayed to God that His provision would be ample to satisfy their energy and hunger needs. The Scriptures are our daily spiritual manna.

The more time we spend consuming The Word of God, the better we get to know Him. The more time spent reading the Word of God, the greater our appetite for the Scriptures. It will be an appetite that is characterized by passionate cravings for God's relationship to us.

## An Excuse To Celebrate

When one particular new king of Judah began his reign, it signaled a change of character (or perhaps a change of heart) from numerous evil kings that had insulted God in so many ways. This new King Josiah didn't have the best upbringing or example as he was growing up. His evil father, King Amon had led the people into idolatry, and his grandfather, King Manasseh, was even worse. King Josiah began his reign at eight years old and probably didn't realize that God had planned his life well in advance. At age 26, King Josiah decided to go all out in renovating the Temple. Was the Temple to become a legacy of his or did he receive a call? After organizing the money for the repairs of the Temple, the message of the Scriptures quickly changes from building construction to an emphasis on the <u>reconstruction of people</u>.

In the process of preparing for the Temple renovation, the High Priest, Hilkiah, discovered a scroll in the Temple with God's laws written on it. He gives the scroll to Josiah's secretary. "Look what I found." Ultimately, King Josiah hears God's laws read and realizes the disinterest by numerous generations of God's people. He grieves over this, but he also determines that the people under his reign will be reacquainted with The Word which had been "lost." Was the lost Word truly lost in being thrown into some insignificant closet, or was The Word lost because of neglect and therefore why have it out if it was not going to be used? With great enthusiasm, King Josiah gathers his people together and reads the entire book of God's laws to them. He further calls for his people to participate in a Passover celebration more festive than any past celebration. Josiah was motivated to celebrate the rediscovery of The Word (See 2 Kings 22; 23:21-22).

As we are the Temple of The Holy Spirit, we can look forward to the coming celebration of revealed truths as we discover or rediscover, as the case may be, the power of The Word. Reconstruct us, Lord God. May we never neglect or hide Your Word again.

There is an exciting incident where The Word changed the "down in the dumps" demeanor and dismal preoccupation of two of Jesus' followers (See Luke 24:13-17). The resurrection had already occurred, but the physical body was missing. These two followers were walking dejectedly to Emmaus and lamenting the death of the One they had hoped would be the glorious Messiah that would come to rescue Israel. Suddenly, Jesus joins them in their walk but they didn't recognize him. Perhaps God kept it from them.

> Then Jesus quoted them passage after passage from the writings of the prophets, beginning with the Book of Genesis and going right on through the Scriptures, explaining what the passages meant and what they said about Himself (Luke 24:27).

As their journey was ending toward Emmaus, they invited Jesus to come home with them. Jesus accepted their invitation. They sat down to eat, and Jesus asked God's blessing on the food. He broke the bread and passed it around. It was then that they realized that The Resurrected Christ was with them (See Luke 24:30-31). Was it only the broken, blessed bread or had God planted a gifted discernment of the earlier quoted Word? I feel the two dejected followers liked what they heard Jesus cite in The Word, and therefore were moved to offer Jesus their hospitality. Jesus accepted because He was not yet finished with the two. The Scriptures (See Luke 24:32) tell us that, "their hearts had felt strangely warm as He talked with them and explained the Scripture during the walk down the road."

The two followers gave their uplifted testimony in excitement. While the breaking of the bread was a major realization in their renewed recognition of Him, I believe that they put two and two together and rejoiced that Christ had made Himself known through the Word.

I can assure you. Like the two travelers/followers on the road to wherever, we will be changed and allowed to see Jesus, The Christ. Father God has planned it that Way. Our very act of turning to God's Word for comfort, hope, encouragement, and wisdom is evidence of our invitation to Jesus to come into our hearts and raise us up.

## Language Issues

Languages change. The archaic King James (English 1611) version of the Bible certainly is not the easiest to understand. Numerous interpretations and commentaries expound on the Scriptures. Purposeful translations with different motives using the original Greek or Hebrew come available.

Biblical scholars and some preachers go to their Hebrew and Greek textbooks to look up the "true" meaning of words in order to get the "right" message. These Hebrew and Greek textbook tools are sometimes used as accuracy battering irons to beat down conflicting revelations received by other people. Most often, the extracted "real" meaning from the original Hebrew and Greek is accepted by those who are less skilled in using a foreign language dictionary.

On the internet one can find an entry enticing one to learn Hebrew in just 10 days. I have not tried that and probably will not.

Timothy S. Morton ("The Greek Game", Internet) questions, "Who should you believe?" after documenting that there are over thirty compiled Greek texts and over 100 English translations, and no two read the same. He refers to those who love to flaunt the Greek as the "Greek addicts." So, dear scholar, which Greek are you using? Is it #1 or #30? Often New Testament writers quote a text from the Old Testament and then "amplify" the meaning in a paraphrase manner to help get the message across. Dick France (The Old Testament in the New Testament, *Zondervan Handbook of the Bible* 743) also points out that the language source differences affect interpretations. As an example, the New Testament writers base their writings on the Greek Septuagint text which sometimes gives different meaning from the Hebrew Old Testament.

There is history of Biblical paraphrasing and commentary before *The Living Bible*. An example are the Aramaic targums. It is thought that translations of the Old Testament into Aramaic "allowed" much additional information. One speculation is that the Aramaic translation was used to signal that it was not original scripture but only commentary and paraphrase. When the Aramaic was read, people knew it was not the original Hebrew. Preachers paraphrase to get their message across each week.

Now that I have used *The Living Bible* (TLB 1971) the past five years, I find background about this paraphrased Bible. I read that it is occasionally remembered and was written by a Baptist layman named Kenneth N. Taylor (1917-2005) in an effort to help his own children and the less educated better understand the Scriptures. Taylor revealed that his efforts to simplify the Scriptures were paraphrases of the American Standard Version (1901). Evangelist, Billy Graham's Crusades brought the paraphrase into prominence during the 1970's. Very few scholars have encouraged its use particularly as a "study Bible". Some have strictly warned against it. Would too many people start understanding? My own recent pastor as well as a few others have from time to time made me feel uneasy when I read it aloud during Bible study. They feel the writer has, "taken too much liberty", in the wording of the passages. I used to let it bother me, but I no longer do. In 1989, Taylor assembled a team of 90 Greek and Hebrew scholars in a project to revise The Living Bible with the intent of retaining the ease of reading of its predecessor but with the added advantage of having been translated from the original Greek and Hebrew sources. Their work resulted in *The New Living Translation* (Tyndale House Publishers 1996). In the meantime, Eugene H. Peterson had published *The Message, The Bible In Contemporary Language* (November 1993). It was featured as, "a contemporary rendering of the Bible from the original language, crafted to present its tone, rhythm, events, and ideas in everyday language." Peterson's call to enhance people's interest in and consumption of God's Word in everyday language is loaded with humility. Too many critics with their "scholarly" astuteness may be abundantly judgmental about the paraphrasing attempts. Peterson writes in his rendering of 1 Peter 5, 2216, "God has had it with the proud, but takes delight in just plain people."

<u>Lord Speak To Me</u>       (Frances     Havergal
                              1836-1879;   Robert
                              Schumann 1810-1856;
                              See Fettke #450)

O use me, Lord, use even me, just as Thou wilt, and when, and where, until Thy blessed face I see— Thy rest, Thy joy, Thy glory share.

Heavenly Father, I want to be among your "plain people". I want You to use me as you continue assembling Your book with its purpose being to glorify You and encourage all to have a daily QT.

Yes, language can put us out of touch, but when we read what He has written, His Word never fails to burst through as The Truth for our every need.

71

Thank you, Father. <u>Prayer</u>: Good Morning, Dear Father. Guide us through a daily understanding of Your Word in such a way that we can't put The Book down. Let The Holy Spirit give us encouragement as we excitedly find ourselves in the Scriptures and realize that it is not just a coincidence. Protect us from any hindrances that would shut us out of Your Word. Let us never feel too full of God's Word, but instead always hungry. In Jesus' precious name, Amen.

# CHAPTER 5

# THE MUSIC
# OF THE SPHERES

Music has always been a part of my life. My mother was the church organist for 35 years. My wife's grandmother was the choir director. I sang in the church choir because my wife to be did when we were dating. My parents "made" me go to various civic music association concerts that were sponsored in our town. I joined the school band in the 9th grade and continued through my senior year. I "played" an alto saxophone that had been used by my father in a community band. It was silver (everyone else had a new gold lacquered one). Can't help throwing this in right here and now – I'd rather have Jesus than silver and gold. Anyway, it was silver. My father had it resilvered and new pads installed so that it looked new when I started. It not only looked new, but it was the only silver one in the whole saxophone section. Fifty-five years ago I eagerly sat for the first time with my reconditioned instrument before the band director who would eventually influence and turn me into a second part player. Like my instrument, I was to learn many years later that my intimacy with God would recondition my life. Early on, I recall the band director verbally reflect that to him, the sound of a saxophone reminded him of the "sound of the devil." Wouldn't you know it. The director loved the percussion people. Now that I think about it, maybe he meant beginning saxophone virtuosos sounded like the devil.

I always had certain favorite hymns, but it was only the melody and not the words that had meaning. Although I realized the hymns were based on scriptures it was meaningless because I didn't know the scriptures. As the QT progressed, the words became more meaningful, and praying the thought behind those words became a treasure of thought and revelations of God's messages. I learned later that it was called, "Praying the Scriptures".

In the Foreword of *The Hymnal for Worship and Celebration* (Fettke 1986), Charles R. Swindoll writes, "If you don't love to sing, then why in the world would you ever want to go to heaven." The hymns began their further stimulation as they impressed on me the value of their teaching and worshipful purpose. Before, it was just the act of singing, but now the ballooning revelations came as the hymns highlighted The Word. All of those talented composers of music and words had become a part of that great crowd watching to see us use what The Holy Spirit had written through them and leave for us as worship tools.

> Since we have such a huge crowd of men watching us from the grandstands, let us strip off anything that slows us down or holds us back—(Hebrews 12:1).

It is as if these saints are saying, "Why don't you use that hymn that I wrote in the lesson you are teaching?" Or maybe some are asking, "Have you ever thought about how my hymn can help you understand God's Word?"

More and more the hymns became of greater importance as a result of my spiritual growth in the QT. Kenneth W. Osbeck has written a book (*Amazing Grace* 1990) in which he assembles the biographies of many inspiring hymn writers. It reveals the background behind the birthing of their compositions and the beautiful variety of ways that God orchestrated their spiritual journey leading to His creation through them.

A major revelation in my increased awareness of the hymns was the unexpected discovery that the composers seemed to speak in favor of and encourage the QT. For me, an early riser, the beginning of each new day was best for the QT. Let me encourage you to adopt the beginning of each new day for the QT. The truth expressed by the secular lyrics, "Start the day with a song and nothing can go wrong" can lead us into the realization that starting each day with The Heavenly Father has extraordinary advantages. In spite of things that normally might overwhelm us, we are bolstered in the assurance that He will not let us be strained beyond what we can endure with His backing and support. We can be armored by His Power.

> But remember this—the wrong desires that come into your life aren't new or different. Many others have faced exactly the same problems before you. And no temptation is irresistible. You can trust God to keep the temptation from becoming so strong that you can't stand up against it, for He has promised this and will do what He says. He will show you how to escape temptation's power so that you can bear up patiently against it (1 Corinthians 10:13).

So how does one start the day during the QT with a song? Outside my window I hear small sparrows chirping as each new day arrives. I am not linguistically talented enough to interpret what their chirps are saying, although on occasion I have counted their chirping patterns. I am convinced that they somehow are so appreciative of the new day that they, in their own way, offer their herald of its arrival.

A favorite hymn recognizes the sparrow's contribution of praise as they give God glory.

This is my Father's world,
The birds their carols raise,
The morning light, the lily white,
Declare their Makers praise.
(Text: Maltbie D. Babcock 1858-1901; Music: Franklin L. Sheppard 1852-1930; See Fettke #58)

And so dear reader, if the birds can do it, so can we. In fact, if I am not mistaken, Jesus had a fondness for the sparrows.

Alright, the birds are earlier risers than I am sometimes. Our QT "transactions" may still be clouded somewhat by the grogginess of the sometimes inadequate sleep. Often, I seem to be prompted by the need to voice some of the words from the hymn, Crown Him With Many Crowns (Matthew Bridges 1800-1894; See Fettke #234)

Awake my soul and sing of Him who died for thee.

Just as we have favorite songs, I wonder if God has favorite songs. I think He does. I believe one of His favorites is the one we sing telling Him how much we love Him.

More love to Thee, O Christ. More love to
Thee!
Hear Thou the prayer I make on bended
knee;
This is my earnest plea: More love, O Christ
to Thee
More love to Thee!

(Text: Elizabeth Prentice 1818-1878; Music: William
H. Doan 1823-1915; See Fettke #363)

<u>Prayer</u>: Heavenly Father, Let our devotion to You
and our daily thoughts about You be motivated with
a desire for an ever increasing love for You. You are
our everything, and we want to start each day with a
new song of love. In His Precious Name, Amen

Obviously we don't necessarily break into song
during each mornings QT. For some of us, it would
not contribute much to quietness. We can, however,
think the words that we might sing, and we don't have
to sing the same song over and over. The Scriptures
in numerous places instruct us to sing a <u>new song</u>.

Sing a new song to the Lord!
Sing it everywhere around the world!
Sing out His praises!
Bless His Name.

Each day tell someone that He saves (Psalm 96:1-2).

---

Sing a new song to the Lord
Telling about His mighty deeds!
For He has won a mighty victory

By His power and holiness. (Psalm 98:1)

---

Sing a new song to the Lord;
Sing His praises, all you who
live in earth's remotest corners!
Sing, O sea! Sing, all of you
who live in distant lands beyond
the sea (Isaiah 42:10).

There is a mystery in this new song that I will

not attempt to investigate other than to comment on

Matthew Henry's reflections (1991 P 883). Perhaps it

would sound like a riddle to us. The riddle goes like

this: When does a new song become old? Answer: It

doesn't when it is a song singing praises to The Living

God. It is always new as each new day is new.

> I love You, Lord and I lift my voice
> To worship You, O my soul rejoice!
> Take joy, my King in what You hear.
> May it be a sweet, sweet sound in
> Your ear.

(Laurie Klein 1978, 1980, House of Mercy Maranatha
Music; See Fettke #80)

# CHAPTER 6

# LOVE AND COMMUNION

<u>Knocking For Love</u>

In our pre-puberty and early pubescent life there are those blissful moments of falling in love with another close to our age or even older than our age. I can remember one of the games played at parties when I was young. It was called, Knock For Love. The parent hosts of the party put all the girls in one room behind a closed door with all the boys lined up outside the shut door. The girls would line up on their side of the shut door. Each boy would knock on the door one at a time and when the door was opened, the girl next in line was the one that the boy who had knocked got to walk around the block with (preferably while holding hands). Of course, there were manipulations of this "social mixer" in both lines in hopes of a strategic pairing with the "right" match. Hopefully, the surprise was matching up with the one you had a crush on.

Those early "love" moments progressively accounted for much time spent in getting to know the one of interest better and better. Sometimes it took the form of holding hands and feeling the tactile wonder. Sometimes it took the form of gifting the opposite sex with candy or the very rare bubble gum which was scarce during World War II. Later it was being a little closer when dancing. Yes, it included writing love notes which were secretly passed to each other, often through a third party.

Ultimately, as I began dating the one that would become my wife, I planted my first kiss on her cheek after our thirteenth date. She used to kid me and tell me she was beginning to wonder if something was wrong with her. You might say I was shy, slow, or didn't know just how to go about it. Boldness was not one of my strengths. I was and am a very serious person.

It is amazing how our spiritual journey with The Heavenly Father parallels our youthful love experiences. The intimacy develops as we get to know Him better and better. That is one power of the QT. God invites us to know him and get better acquainted.

I don't want your sacrifices – I want your
love
I don't want your offering – I want you to
know me

(Hosea 6:6)

The words of the song, Getting To Know You

(The King and I 1951) perfectly describe the progres-

sion of communion with God that the QT fosters.

<u>GETTING TO KNOW YOU</u>

Getting to know you
Getting to know all about you
Getting to like you
Getting to hope you like me.
Getting to know you.
Getting to feel free and easy
When I am with you
Getting to know what to say.
Haven't you noticed
Suddenly I'm bright and breezy?
Because of all the beautiful and new
Things I'm learning about you.
Day—by—Day

The youthful experiences with the like/love

progression now reveal themselves as early manifestations of what our spiritual journey can develop into. Is that God's plan? I believe it is. Recalling the Knock For Love game, we see Jesus encouraging this knock for love activity, and amazingly it works on both sides of the door.

> And so it is with prayer—keep on looking and asking and you will keep on finding; knock and the door will be opened (Luke 11:9-10).

---

> Look! I have been standing at the door and I am constantly knocking. If anyone hears me calling and opens the door, I will come and fellowship with him and he with me! (Revelation 3:20).

Both are blessed assurances and in effect, Promises.

Getting to know our one of interest suggests God's Plan that entices us to want to know Him better. And paralleling the song, Getting To Know

You, we get to feel the excitement as we incorporate the daily QT into our schedules. The progression moves from liking. We hope that God likes us. As we get to know Him better we feel free and easier in His Presence. We learn how to tell Him that we love Him, and we get tongue-tied less often in our prayers. Because He allows us to experience more and more of His creative and mysterious depths, we get giddy with exhilarating spiritual experiences that flood our awareness at times. As the song says, we truly become bright and breezy day-by-day. If we devote ourselves to the QT each day, it will happen.

No Longer A Stranger

Walking around the block holding hands with your one of interest was sometimes purposely prolonged. One block just wasn't enough. The song, "Stranger In Paradise" (Musical, Kismet 1953) lyrics could describe the desire of the searching, devoted lover who is consumed beyond all rational rapture for the Lord God Almighty, our Beautiful Redeeming Savior, Jesus Christ, and the Holy Spirit.

> Take my hand, I'm a stranger in paradise
> All lost in a wonderland
> A stranger in paradise

———————

> If I stand starry-eyed
> That's the danger in paradise
> For mortals who stand beside an angel like
>         you.
> Won't you answer this fervent prayer
> Of a stranger in paradise
> Don't send me in dark despair
> From all that I hunger for
> But open your angel's arms
> To this stranger in paradise
> And tell him that he need be
> A stranger no more.

Many of us feel as though we are strangers in paradise. It is a strange new place for some of us to visit, and we may feel at first as though we are wandering aimlessly without a tour guide. Tours often provide for private, free time for the travelers so that they may gather their individual thoughts and rest from the often dazzling personal experiences and stimuli. God's Paradise is where He is, and He is always interested when we show an interest in taking a spiritual tour around the block. He wants to hold our hand and not only be our guide, but also to take the lead.

> O Jesus, I have promised
> To serve Thee to the end;
> Be Thou, forever near me
> My Master and my Friend;
> I shall not fear the battle If
> Thou art by my side,

Nor wander from the pathway
If Thou wilt be my guide.
(Text: John E. Bode 1816-1874; Music: Arthur H. Mann 1850-1929; See Fettke #369)

Being starry-eyed in God's paradise is not dangerous. The more hungry we are to know Him better, the more He feeds us with discernment and revelation.

So many times we search for the right gift to bestow on our loved one. That which is the tangible given is what we want to be an extension and remembrance of ourselves. Our beautiful Savior, Jesus Christ, is like that. The Father came to earth as a man to bestow the gift of eternal life on all who accept and love Him. He wants to be remembered for His gift to us. Oswald Chambers (*My Utmost For His Highest* June 13) reminds us about gifts.

"We have the idea that we can dedicate our gifts to God. However, you cannot dedicate what is not yours. There is actually only one thing you can dedicate to God, and that is your right to yourself".

I Love You The Best

As a small child, my mother engaged me in jovial verbal banter regarding the word, LOVE. I still remember the sequence:

Mother    -"I love you."
Me        -"I love you too."
Mother    -"I love you the best."
Me        -"No, I love you the best."
Mother    -(very rapidly spoken) "You always say you love me the best, but I love you the best.

We would then burst into laughter and relish in the words of love for each other. Many years later when I approached her hospital bed where she lay in a semi-coma condition and could barely talk, I greeted her with the words, "I love you." She barely spoke but did so with the words above reversed in the sequence. Those were her last words spoken to me, and yet I knew that she knew I had come.

Now I realize her message in "love dialogue" was that you cannot "outlove" me. Neither can we "outlove" our Blessed Savior. We must never find it too difficult to say these three words, "I Love You."

## Beyond Friendship

After breakfast Jesus said to Simon Peter, "Simon, son of John, do you love me more than the others?" "Yes", Peter replied, "You know I am your friend." "Then feed my lambs", Jesus told him. Jesus repeated the question: "Simon, son of John, do you really love me"? "Yes, Lord", Peter said, "you know I am your friend." "Then take care of my sheep". Jesus said. Once more he asked him, "Simon, son of John, are you even my friend?" Peter was grieved at the way Jesus asked the question this third time. "Lord, you know my heart; you know I am", he said. Jesus said, "Then feed my little sheep."

(John 21:15-17)

It seems to me that Peter felt a closeness to Jesus but still couldn't quite say the three words, I Love You that Jesus was seeking. I am aware that there is controversy relative the Greek of this translation as it contrasts the "agape" love with the "phileo" love. But, at least we can consider Peter's progressive love for His Savior. Perhaps it was a progressive thing for Peter as it is for us. Later on Peter seems to track the progression of love without embarrassment. It's almost as though Peter had spent time in the QT when he wrote:

Do you want more and more of God's kindness and peace? Then learn to know Him better and better. For as you know Him better, He will give you through His great power, everything you need for living a truly good life; He even shares His own glory and His own goodness with us! (2 Peter 1:2-4).

Peter then further speaks of the progressive communion with God:

> — —you must learn to know God better and discover what He wants you to do. Next, learn to put aside your own desires so that you will become patient and godly, gladly letting God have His way with you. This will make possible the next step which is for you to enjoy people and to like them, and finally you will grow to love them deeply. The more you go on in this way, the more you will grow strong spiritually and become fruitful and useful to our Lord Jesus Christ (2 Peter 1:5-8)

Just as Peter progressed from LIKE to LOVE, we too follow the same steps in our spiritual journey with our Wonderful Tour Guide who give us exquisite glimpses of Himself in the QT.


It Takes Two To Tango (Ballroom, That Is)

In some of our youthful days the thought of drawing nearer to our dance partner was not always reality, but still it certainly was imagined and antici-pated as a possibility. One of the popular television programs of recent times capitalizes on interest in intricate dance movements. These movements are skillfully choreographed and the judging of the performance is very competitive. Some dancing partners are not good enough. Some win, and some lose. Two beautiful people in the church I attend are John and Shirley Poteet. Knowing that Shirley taught dancing as a university physical education associate professor at Trinity University in San Antonio, Texas, I asked her to brainstorm on the parallels of dance and Christianity. She graciously responded in such a beautiful way by "seeing" the spiritual in the secular. Shirley's list could become a small group study in itself. Meditate a bit on this. First, let your thoughts reflect on defining the secular aspects. Then let the spiritual message that God has for you become a revelation of His Presence. And further, seek evidence in God's Word that justifies your discernment.

1. You must have a partner.

   Question: What attributes would you include in choosing a partner?

2. You must have a leader and a follower.

   Question: Who determines who the leader will be and who the follower will be?

3. You must journey/move in sync with your partner.

   Question: Does the journey destination depend on joint efforts?

4. Follower must yield to cues/direction of the leader.

Question: How does the leader communicate

directions to the follower?

5. There is joy in moving together in rhythm.

Question: What enhances the rhythm of

togetherness?

6. There is a pattern that emerges in choreog-

raphy/the way you live your life.

Question: Have you sought the best talent

to choreograph your life or are you

self-indulged?

7. There is patience-tolerance-respect required in

learning a dance.

Question: What attributes of learning a dance

are applicable to living a Christian life?

8. There is a balance required in dance.

Question: How do we maintain our balance and keep from falling?

9. Leadership comes from the core—in dance, the physical core (the torso).

Question: How does one become the respected leader with a healthy spiritual core?

10. We must be trusting and trustworthy.

Question: What contributes to mutual trust between two dancers in perfect Spiritual harmony?

11. Partnership is established by invitation and acceptance.

Question: What is the proper RSVP to the invitation?

12. Begins with basics and stays true to basics as the underlying principle.

<u>Question</u>: What basics must remain constant in our spiritual journey?

13. Focus

<u>Question</u>: What hindrances interrupt our focus?

<u>Summary</u>: If you treated your neighbor as a dance you would have: respect, harmony, balance, trust, precision, affection, growth, comprehension, inspiration, no pushing or pulling, no antagonism.

Dance, then, wherever you may be;
I am the Lord of the Dance, said he,
And I'll lead you all, wherever you may be,
And I'll lead you all in the dance, said he.
(Sydney Carter, Lord of the Dance 1963)

Thank you Shirley. May the Lord of the Dance be your partner! Thank you, John, for being Shirley's partner as one in Christ.

The youthful love notes written to the significant other were a combination of one's daily activity blended with carefully worded elements of love and affection inserted to keep the "fires burning", just in case that the significant other might be attracted or inclined to another suitor. Sometimes we write our prayers to God. Sometimes we pray The Scriptures – meaning "copying" the thoughts of what The Holy Spirit has inspired others to write. Sometimes we pray our love notes by sending them to The Heavenly Father through a third party – our Savior Jesus Christ who is our Spokesperson and Who intercedes for us to The Father.

> He is able to save completely all who come to God through him. Since he will live forever, he will always be there to remind God that he has paid for their sins with his blood (Hebrews 7:25).

Just Give It Time

Take time to be holy. Oswald Chambers (*My Utmost For His Highest*, June 13) guides us with these words:

> "If you will give God your right to yourself, He will make a holy experiment out of you – and His experiments always succeed. Never try to make your experience a principle for others, but allow God to be as creative and original with others as He is with you."

The QT is the time for being holy. How can we become holy? Allow the words of the hymn, Take Time To Be Holy (Text: William D. Longstaff 1822-1894; Music: George C. Stebbins 1846-1945. See Fettke #441) to give us direction.

> Speak oft with thy Lord;
> Abide in Him always and
> Feed on His Word.
> Make Friends of God's children;
> Help those who are weak;

Seek His blessing for all things;
Spend much time in secret with Jesus alone;
Let Him be thy guide;
Be calm in thy soul.

Quiet moments alone with God allow Him to restore our soul (See Psalm 23:1-3). We have to get used to letting Him teach us how to be still. The QT is that time that we take to be holy. Don't let that important time pass you. It is a time that will stand and give you bonus hours beyond the normal twenty four.

# CHAPTER 7

# SPIRITURAL

—◦◦◦—

You got a later start, Robert, but there is still hope. You can always restart the Spring of life where everything each new day is bright and new. Am I talking of myself? Am I trying to console myself? Am I trying to find a reason to excuse myself? An unknown poet has penned The Fifth Season which consoles some as it is often used as an end of life comfort thought for the family.

> But with the passing of these seasons, Life
> is still not done, not through,
> For there is yet another season,

When each spirit is renewed.
And it is in this calm fifth season,
A time of cleansing and rebirth,
A time of new awakening — —.

My high school principal had a favorite Scripture that he used to read frequently in assemblies. Yes, they used to read the Bible in school. It was the long list of "times" that was prefaced by the statement, "There is a right time for everything"— (See Ecclesiastes 3:1). The students endured as he periodically read the twenty-seven "times, although we were pretty well traumatized by the second verse – A time to be born, a time to die. If only he had read a little further, we would have been encouraged by the fact that there is a right time for everything and those right times are historically repeated in each of our lives, but the times are initially planned by The Creator for His creations.

In my season (is it the Fifth?) I sought The Lord. I began the QT. Was it too late? Definitely not, and I suspect that the later you start the more accelerated the blessings come and the greater the regret that an earlier daily communion with God was not started.

From my viewpoint, let me encourage you to focus on the accelerated blessings regardless of the season and disregard the regret of not starting sooner. The take action time, NOW, is more important than the past seasons.

## Growing By Leaps Or Bounds

Father, can it be that I am experiencing You? Do everyday secular things take on new meanings that are spiritual? Yes, as we get to know God more intimately in the QT, we become more alert to the fact that God is in every circumstance of our life. As we spend more time with our Creator, we progressively begin to sense His Presence in everything. I believe that is the way He planned it (us). I cannot say that everyone's spiritual maturity grows at the same rate, but I can promise you that a major reason for the QT is that it helps us to grow spiritually. Oswald Chambers (*My Utmost For His Highest* May 18) reminds us that, "Jesus said there is only one way to develop and grow spiritually and that is through focusing and concentrating on God." His April 18 devotional entry alerts us to "be ready for the sudden surprise visits of God." Chambers also writes of our daily opportunity to experience God. "Each morning as you awake there is a new opportunity to go out, building your confidence in God." (January 2) The deeper our intimacy with God grows, the less surprised we are by The Holy Spirit.

Manifestation of The Holy Spirit occurs in increasingly vivid ways. One of the most enjoyable ways is His leading us into surprise visits of spiritual awareness. For an exciting experience, let me suggest that you read Jack Deere's two books, *Surprised By The Power Of The Spirit* and *Surprised By The Voice Of God* (Prince Press, 2003). The Spirit's surprise visits become increasingly more frequent in the QT and outside the QT.

Let me give you just a few examples of everyday things that have taken on spiritual meaning for me. Letting my mind wander as I notice a projector screen with tripod legs—Oh, the Holy Trinity! Seeing the scoreboard in the gymnasium that says

"Home" and "Visitors". We are just visitors here. Home is elsewhere.

## Spiritual Nutrition

The advertisement on the outside of a Quaker Life cereal box reads and grabs my attention: "Helps promote <u>healthy hearts</u>. Quaker Life is the perfect start to your best days. Embrace life each day with just the right <u>sweetness</u> and <u>trusted nutrition</u>. Look at life in a new <u>way</u>." The QT will do what the cereal box speaks of

> Create in me a new, clean heart, O God,
> Filled with clean thoughts and right desires
>     (Psalm 51:10)

The spiritual nutrition of consuming The Word of God provides the sweetness for facing each new day.

'Tis so sweet to trust in Jesus, Just to

Take Him at His word, Just to rest upon His
   promise.
Just to know "Thus saith the Lord". Jesus,
Jesus, how I trust Him!
How I've proved Him o'er and o'er! Jesus,
Jesus, precious Jesus!
O for grace to trust Him more.
(Text: Louisa M. R. Stead, 1850-1917; Music: William
J. Kirkpatrick, 1838-1921; See Fettke #350).

Looking, at LIFE (cereal or otherwise) in a new

way makes each day a new one when He is our

beginning and when we recognize Him as the Way

we want to go.

Jesus told him (speaking to Thomas), "I am
the Way – yes, and the truth and the Life"
(John 14:6).

Just one more example. Many times families

purchase bed linens that are themed as a way to

please their children or grandchildren. We had long

ago purchased some bed sheets that had hearts with

Valentine sayings. One morning as I was getting on

my knees (the posture is your choice) along the side of the bed with the Valentine sheets, my eyes caught the heart with the words, "I love you". To me, God was speaking through the bed sheets, and my spontaneous remark was, "I love You too, Lord." Two other hearts had spiritually meaningful words: "Be Mine" and "I'm Yours".

Too juvenile? I think not. At least God lets me see things at times that are exciting. I know. As I track some of my spiritual growth experiences in this book, I am cautioned not to overpower the reader with where I have been or where I am now. It's the journey and the beauty of the landscape that counts. Edwin B. Young (*Praying For Keeps*. 10) cautions us about the natural tendency we will have to advertise the great change in our lives. "We will want to start dropping little comments to let other people know that we have regular appointments with the King of the universe". Jesus, I know you instructed us to go into the secret, private, quiet place, but finding You there is just so exciting I can't help but share with others.

When Jesus healed the two blind men, He sternly warned them not to tell anyone about it, but instead, they spread His fame all over town (See Matthew 9:27-31). I believe Jesus knew the two healed ones could not refrain from sharing the good news of how He had changed their lives. Likewise, as Jesus was ascending to heaven, He told the disciples, "Don't begin telling others yet—stay here in the city until The Holy Spirit comes and fills you with power from heaven" (Luke 24:49). Perhaps Jesus wants us to have the strongest relationship possible with Him before we try to tell others about the availability of that relationship.

One time I used the word, "spiritual" and my pastor asked me what I meant by spiritual. I took his question as a way to be certain he understood what I was speaking of. My response, at that time, was that it meant having to do with God and an intimate relationship with Him enhanced by the QT and a point in one's journey when there are times when The Holy Spirit's manifest presence is recognized. I didn't know if the pastor thought I had enough theological understanding or not, but he didn't say any more. I had surprised myself by my ready answer without stammering in trying to utter it. I had often prayed during the QT for The Holy Spirit to think my thoughts, speak my words, and act my acts. He will honor that prayer.

There were rare times that my prayers surprised me. After my "Amen", I thought to myself, did I say that? Was I learning? Was I being taught?

> But you dear friends, must build up your lives ever more strongly upon the foundation of our holy faith, learning to pray in the power and strength of the Holy Spirit (Jude 1:20).

I had read about The Holy Spirit helping us in prayer even when we didn't know what to say, and I wanted that kind of prayer power although I realized it was not to be my prayer power, but that of The Holy Spirit. Again, the Book of Romans speaks.

> And in the same way—by our faith—the Holy Spirit helps us with our daily problems and in our praying. For we don't even know what we should pray for, nor how to pray as we should; but the Holy Spirit prays for us

with such feeling that it cannot be expressed
in words (Romans 8:26-28).

My spiritual growth was progressing because
I was following one of the prescribed physical
therapies which had payoffs in spiritual ways. The
physical therapy was called the QT. The payoffs
were coming in the form of spiritual maturity and
understanding of God's Way. The Apostle, Paul, had
already written his advice to the young Timothy:

> Spend your time and energy in the exercise
> of keeping spiritually fit. Bodily exercise is
> all right, but spiritual exercise is much more
> important and is a tonic for all you do (1
> Timothy 4:7-8).

Ask your cardiologist his opinion of this Scripture
sometime.

A final narrative about my spiritual journey is the
movement of God in the life of my marriage. My
wife had begun her QT awhile back. Early on, at

times she would express concern over whether or not she was experiencing The Holy Spirit's presence. I kept telling her that she would. I will just say that she did. God honors all who seek His Presence. Earlier, I had read a book (no longer in print) by David and Jan Stoop. The book, *When Couples Pray Together* (Regal Books, 2000) stimulated an enhancement of the QT in a marriage whereby husband and wife could expand their individual quiet times into a joint replication. I asked my wife to read the book and then tell me if she wanted to have a joint time of prayer together. She read the book, and we began our joint quiet time with God on May, 2007. We regrettably missed one day because we forgot, but no more. For any pastor called on to offer marital counseling, I think one of their first strategies should be to strongly suggest that the couples pray together. Unfortunately, the Stoops have found, "in talking to many pastors and their wives that couples in the ministry probably don't pray together any more often than do those in their congregation. It is a 4% statistic. It takes courage to get started. Spouses are supposed to be as one. Praying with your spouse every day enhances that oneness with The One who causes no jealousy.

> Then Jesus told him (the blind man He had healed), "I have come into the world to give sight to those who are spiritually blind to show those who think they see that they are blind" (John 9:39).

Prayer: Heavenly Father, Cure me of all my spiritual blindness and use me to encourage others to look for and see the spiritual in the everyday secular. In His Precious Name, Amen

# CHAPTER 8

# DISCERNED TRUTHS

———◦◦◦———

This section of the book is about some of the things that I believe God has shared with me. I have chosen to call these discerned truths. Before I share some of these discerned truths, I first want to emphasize that they are truths that have personally been shared with me and for me. They may have already been discerned by you in some way if you have already embarked on the daily QT. God has His Way of individualizing these truths.

It's My Turn

At the beginning, I asked the question, "Who's quiet time is it"? I previously mentioned the monologue versus the dialogue issue. I progressed to the awareness that it was not just my QT, but His QT with me also. Since I didn't successfully handle the listening part of my monologue, I believe God chose His QT to be at night. Many times I am awakened and flooded with thoughts that I believe are definite things that God has to say to me. It's as though He is saying, "It's my turn. Now hear Me out." At times I have thought to myself (as though God does not know my thoughts) that I would prefer it if He could talk to me during the first part of the day. As He is a merciful God, I think that He would "comply" if I could improve my listening skills and diminish my talking skills. Of course, the advantage would be that I would experience a better nights

sleep. This issue has partially been compensated for by

the realization that God has a purpose for waking me

during the night. That purpose promoted me to start

asking, "Dear Father, is there something or someone

You want me to pray about?" I can assure you that

almost immediately after asking Him that question, He

gives the prayer assignment, and when the prayer is

over, sleep is restored (most of the time).

> —but one night after Eli had gone to bed
> (he was almost blind with age by now), and
> Samuel was sleeping in the Temple near the
> Ark, the Lord called out, "Samuel! Samuel!"
> "Yes?" Samuel replied. What is it? He jumped
> up and ran to Eli. "Here I am. What do you
> want?" he asked. "I didn't call you," Eli said.
> "Go on back to bed." So he did. –And the
> Lord came and called as before, "Samuel!
> Samuel!" And Samuel replied, "Yes, I'm
> listening" (1 Samuel 3:2-5; 10).

I will bless the Lord who counsels me; He gives me the wisdom in the night. He tells me what to do (Psalm 16:7).

## Dark Night of the Soul

And speaking of the night, there is a spiritual phenomena that happens to us when we feel uneasily alone spiritually. It is called the Dark Night of the Soul. In the Christian tradition, one who has developed a strong prayer life and consistent devotion to God may at times feel as though God has suddenly abandoned them or that his prayer life has collapsed. This can worsen so that belief is lost in the very existence of God and/or validity of religion. One writer calls it a metaphor for a certain loneliness and desolation. All of this sounds pretty frightening, but lend me your ears (if you are here to let me tell you) and your eyes (if you will read my experiences with the Dark Night of the Soul).

First of all, I am not absolutely certain that I have been involved in the Dark Night of the Soul. That is too theological for me to contemplate. If I have, and it is of God to test my spiritual strength, He has not yet tested me too hard. On the other hand, one of my discerned truths is that the greater the communion intimacy with The Heavenly Father, the more sensitive you are going to be when it seems like the Holy Spirit doesn't seem around like He once was. As the QT brings us closer to our Creator, we feel this absence more keenly when we have done something to displease Him. The more we love Him, the greater we miss Him, and the more we want His Presence back.

For me, I believe that this uneasy Dark Night of the Soul experience is the Holy Spirit's way of letting me know that I have messed up somewhere and He is not pleased with my actions, thoughts, or words. The first time this happened I knew something didn't feel right. Things had been so good and now they didn't feel so good. What was wrong? It took me awhile to pray an inquiry and ask forgiveness for whatever it was that I had done that wasn't pleasing God. Sometimes it took two or three days for God's response to come through, and when it did, by His grace, I was in agreement and realized my errors. In the early stages of my QT, I did not pray an inquiry as to what was wrong and why I felt the uneasy absence or the sense that I had lost a friend.

Show me the path where I should go, O Lord;
point out the right road for me to walk. Lead
me; teach me; for You are the God who gives
me salvation. I have no hope except in You
(Psalm 25:4).

As I progressed in the QT I was able to meditate

about this uneasy feeling of "abandonment" and felt

the ease of realization of guilt and did not have to wait

to pray for the cause. The Holy Spirit speaks quickly

to those who are alert to and attend to His loving

correction. Oswald Chambers (*My Utmost For His

Highest* September 12) speaks of this spiritual confu-

sion as, "The Shrouding of His Friendship."

"Jesus gave the illustration of a man who
appears not to care for his friend (Luke 11:5-
8). He was saying in effect, that is how the
Heavenly Father will appear to you at times.
You think that He is an unkind friend, but
remember He is not. The time will come when
everything will be explained. There seems to
be a cloud on the friendship of the heart, and
often even love itself has to wait in pain and

tears for the blessing of fuller fellowship and oneness."

The dark night times, while uncomfortable, can be a time of God's correction and a time for us to examine ourselves for a self-awareness assisted by the Holy Spirit. The uncomfortable feeling might be discouraging, but let me assure you that something else is about to come in its proper moment. God likes confession and surrender, and when we have done so, He gives us the restored peace that we experienced before the dark night.

The Power of One

Another discerned truth has to do with my wife, Liane. We have celebrated 53 years of married life. We had grown up in the same church that both our parents attended. The minister that married us was also the minister who had baptized us as infants. Talk about a pastor's long-term care! But it was in the QT that I learned to love my wife more each day.

> Anyone who wants to be my follower must love me far more than he does his own father, mother, wife, children, brothers, or sisters— yes, more than his own life—otherwise he cannot be my disciple (Luke 14:26).

This does not mean that a person will not be saved, but it does mean that one cannot be entirely His. Strangely, you would think that following Jesus' stipulation of wanting our love to be channeled to Him and away from our spouse might cause jealousy and all kinds of marital discord. That doesn't happen. In God's magnificent, creative Way, He turns the allegiance to one's spouse into a mightier love than either spouse could ever imagine. This amazing, no jealousy state is arrived at because God planned it that way. His secret surprise for us comes as a result

of the molding of two into one—one whereby both

spouses want the same thing in Christ Jesus.

> This explains why a man leaves his father
> and mother and is joined to his wife in
> such a way that the two become one person
> (Genesis 2:24).

The concept of oneness is providential as a part

of God's plan.

> You were united to your wife by the Lord.
> In God's wise plan, when you married, the
> two of you became one person in his sight
> (Malachi 2:15).

The apostle, Paul, writes with logical reasoning

about this same Oneness.

> For since a man and his wife are now one, a
> man is really doing himself a favor and loving
> himself when he loves his wife (Ephesians
> 5:28).

That oneness is then sealed by the prayer of Jesus Himself as He petitions The Father in our behalf.

> My prayer for all of them is that they will be of one heart and mind, just as you and I are, Father—that just as you are in me and I am in you, so they will be in us, and the world will believe you sent me (John 17:21).

As Oswald Chambers (*My Utmost For His Highest* May 22) pointed out:

> "Jesus prayed nothing less for us than absolute oneness with Himself, just as He was one with the Father.
> Some of us are far from this oneness; yet God will not leave us alone until we are one with Him—because Jesus prayed, 'that they all may be one.'"

I can promise you that your devotion to the QT will draw you closer to the Oneness goal and genuine love will abound.

The Love Formula

There is little doubt that Love and Oneness are closely linked. In fact, the Scriptures express this message over and over. Two revelations come to our hearts. We are to have <u>One Love</u>. "You may worship no other God than me" (Exodus 20:3). We are to <u>Love One</u> (another) – an other.

> And you must love your neighbor just as much as you love yourself (Luke 10:27).

When we <u>have</u> One Love (The Blessed Savior), then we pretty much automatically will love One (another).

> We are <u>one</u> in the Spirit, we are <u>one</u> in the Lord. And they'll know we are Christians by our love, by our love, Yes, they'll know we are Christians by our love.

(Peter Scholtes 1938 – They'll Know We Are Christians by Our Love. Copyright 1966 by F.E.L. Publications; See Fettke #284)

The most important discerned truth is surrender. For some, the idea of surrender smacks of weakness, but when we raise our white flag to The Lord Jesus, we trade our weakness for His strength. The Holy Spirit gradually assists us in surrender. The more I wanted to surrender, the more He helped me to do so. Surrender, for me, means discarding my ways for His Ways and feeling good about it. The more daily QT intimacy occurs, the more daily "all time" intimacy occurs. The song refrain of "You Are Always On My Mind" expresses the deep yearning for the spiritual communion that the QT brings to fruition. Again, I make you another promise. The QT will envelope you with a Godly preoccupation of thought that will cause brain fog to everything else.

Let me encourage you to express the words of surrender found in Judson W. VanDeVenter's hymn, I Surrender All. (See Fettke #366).

All to Jesus I surrender,
All to Him I freely give;
I will ever love and trust Him, In His presence daily live.

All to Jesus I surrender,
Make me Savior, wholly Thine; May The Holy Spirit fill me,
May I know Thy power divine.

All to Jesus I surrender,
Lord, I give myself to Thee;
Fill me with Thy love and power, Let Thy blessing fall on me.

Oswald Chambers (*My Utmost For His Highest* September 13) reminds us that, "God never forces a person's will into surrender, and He never begs. He patiently waits until that person willingly yields to Him."

Betrayed Trust

Early on in the QT, trust becomes an issue. I thought that I was totally trusting in Jesus and, by the way, proudly so. Uh, oh! Let me trace the pattern that happened to me. I say a pattern because I now know that He knows me better than I know myself. I had been offended by a member of the church. I was aware that others in the church didn't prefer this person, but since I was the one who had been personally affected, I prayed to God that I sure would like Him to take care of this. "I turn this over to you, Father." I felt good about doing that. Some days later, I felt inclined to discuss the issue with my pastor "and see what he thought" about the way I had been offended. After I left that meeting with this off my chest, I soon started feeling the dark night type experience. Ultimately, I was convicted by the Holy Spirit's correction. Here's how I remember what the Holy Spirit impressed on me. "You prayed to Me to take the burden off of you. Why didn't you let Me handle it? When you were aggrieved and offended, you asked Me to deal with it and then tried to handle it on your own." And then the correction time came by way of a piercing question. "Didn't you think I knew how?" Discerned truth was received. Forgive me, Lord.

First Things First

Without getting involved in serving others, God's love cannot be given to others. There is an approach to catering to the pre-saved by way of activities within the church premises. It goes something like this. Sponsor some activity and then invite the pre-saved to come witness the joy of God's congregation and see the communion that they enjoy. They will then want to experience the same that they see others experiencing and subject themselves to be discipled by the congregation. That is perhaps a crude or clumsy way of saying what often happens when program (especially non-spiritual, non-Savior focused) offerings take precedent over intimacy and spirituality. One of the failures that I have had has been an inability to convince others that we seem to have our spiritual priorities backwards. As a young teenager, I used to meet on Sunday evenings for youth fellowship. We would eat and sing—eat and sing. One of the songs that we often sang among nonsensical and jovial ones was, "We Are Climbing

Jacob's Ladder." Little did we realize the depth of meaning that the ultimate meaning of the ladder was Christ as we attempt to reach God.

"We are Climbing Jacob's Ladder" has been a refreshing reconnection of my spiritual deficit days with an increased discernment of a more mature awareness of the song. I might say that it has become the theme song (at least the fourth verse) of my vision for Christ's church where I attend and worship. Let me share the words of this Negro spiritual.

> If you love him, why not serve him? If you love him, why not serve him? If you love him, why not serve him?

Soldiers of the cross (Reynolds, Baptist Hymnal #147)

I like that progression. That's the way it should be. When we learn to love Him so intimately, the urge resulting from that deep communion with Him to serve Him cannot be stifled. It just naturally pops out. We can't help it, for He is in control and is The Prompter of all that we do in His Name. We hear people say that many churches are dying. They sponsor numerous activities (the more, the prouder) in hopes of attracting clientele to offerings that might be more appropriate to a school district's adult education program. I believe that the church that I attend, and perhaps others as well, have unwittingly rewritten the words to the Jacob's Ladder song:

If you serve him, why not love him?

To me, that is an opposite progression which may delight Satan as he stimulates this wrongly motivated activity. We must first be prepared by the Holy Spirit before we serve in the name of Jesus. Remember, Jesus instructed His followers to wait—to stay in

Jerusalem until the Holy Spirit had arrived to fill them (Acts 1:4).

Oswald Chambers (*My Utmost For His Highest*) devoted a lot of his time cautioning about this contradictory approach. Please, patiently mediate and digest these cautions. The dates are those of the daily devotions in this book.

"So much Christian work today has never been disciplined, but has come into being by impulse" (September 9).

"Beware of any work for God that causes or allows you to avoid concentrating on Him. A great number of Christian workers worship their work. A worker who lacks this serious controlling emphasis of concentration on God is apt to become overly burdened by his work. Consequently, he becomes burned out and defeated. But the opposite is equally true—once our concentration is on God, all the limits of our life are free and under the control and mastery of God alone. There is no longer any responsibility on you for the work. The only responsibility you have is to stay in living constant touch with God, and to see that you allow nothing to hinder your cooperation with Him" (April 23).

"If you want to be of use to God, maintain the proper relationship with Jesus Christ by staying focused on Him, and He will make use of you every minute you live—yet you will be unaware on the conscious level of your life, that you are being used of Him" (May 18).

"The rallying cry today is, "We must get to work! The heathens are dying without God. We must go and tell them about Him. The purpose of our Christian training is to get us into the right relationship to the 'needs' of God and His will. Once God's 'needs' in us have been met, He will open the way for us to accomplish His will, meeting His 'needs' elsewhere" (May 31).

"We consider what we do in the way of Christian work or service, yet Jesus Christ calls service to be what we are to Him, not what we do for Him" (June 19).

"We can remain powerless by trying to do God's work without concentrating on His power, and by following instead the ideas that we draw from our old nature. We actually slander and dishonor God by our very eagerness to serve Him without knowing Him" (October 3).

"The call of God is not a call to serve Him in any particular way. My contact with the nature of God will shape my understanding of His call and will help me realize what I truly desire to do for Him" (January 17).

"Beware of anything that competes with your loyalty to Jesus Christ. The greatest competitor of true devotion to Jesus is the service we do for Him. It is easier to serve than to pour out our lives completely for Him" (January 18).

I often think that there are not enough people to do all that needs to be done in the life of Christ' church. Perhaps the secret is the empowerment by way of intimate relationship through the QT. No more wondering about one's purpose, no more fatigue and burnout from Christian service with the wrong motive, no more pride and impulsivity dealing with emergency cares, no more worship of the god of work, no more powerless effort with our plans, and no more withholding of self from Him. Build the intimacy with Him Who loves us more than we can ever love Him, and all of these "no mores" will disappear.

<u>Prayer</u>: Heavenly Father, let Your people seek the intimacy of the daily quiet time and in doing so, reap the joy of serving You as You work in us. In His Precious Name, Amen

# CONCLUSION

---

Good Morning, Dear Father. This is the beginning of the end (the last part) or perhaps I should say, the beginning that has no end with You. Like Bob Sorge (*Secrets of the Secret Place.* 194), I too have shared some secrets. Are secrets of the secret place meant to be shared? Yes, if we want to be used by God in encouraging the total church to experience what we are experiencing through the "catalyst" of the QT.

> "The secret place is not the destination; it is only the catalyst. It is designed of God to establish us in an intimate friendship with

Him that is walked out through the course of our everyday lives. The goal we're after is an everyday walk of unbroken communion with our Lord and Friend."

Immersing oneself in the daily QT may seem like a burden if you try it, but don't stop, for if you do, you will miss it. Persevere and God will honor you by drawing closer each day. Don't believe for a minute that pastors and ordained spiritual leaders are the only ones who have a daily QT. Many of them do not. Just be sure that your secret place is free from hindrances and interruptions. Enter the QT with expectation that something is going to change for the better. You will be a new and different person with a fresh newness in all you do and think (See Romans 12:2). Something good is bound to rub off. It did for Peter and John as they preached with enthusiasm. The Jewish Council saw their boldness and could see that they were obviously uneducated non-professionals. They were amazed and realized what being with Jesus had done for them (See Acts 4:13). The QT will enable you to sing that new song.

As a young family we went on a vacation to the Arkansas tourist site called the Crater of Diamonds. Our small children and their parents sat out in the hot sun with spades and hand claws digging for the elusive diamond that would make us rich. We dug with expectation that we were going to find a diamond. We were not concerned what the size of it would be. We just wanted to find one even though it might be brown and opaque instead of shiny and transparent. We dug and dug as the sweat streamed and the sunburn set in. That didn't matter. We were on a quest to find the item of great value. The QT is much like The Crater of Diamonds experience. It takes effort to dig and pray. Unlike the elusive diamond which we did not find, immersion in the QT rewards us with exquisite morsels of value each day that we dig. The devoted effort gradually changes from a short part of our day and crescendos to an open-ended communion that lasts all day every day.

Prayer: Heavenly Father, I am a diamond in the rough. Thank you for finding me. Polish me, Father. Remove all my impurities, and cleave me so that Your Light becomes a brilliance in me. In His Precious Name, Amen.

I have longed for the time when the church where I worship would talk about and stress the QT, but it has not. This is no longer a discouragement to me because the truth of God's Word is always uplifting and encouraging.

> Slowly, steadily, surely, the time approaches when the vision will be fulfilled. If it seems slow, do not despair, for these things will surely come to pass. They will not be overdue a single day! (Habakkuk 2:3).

Ed Young (*Praying For Keeps*, 78) asks the question. "If you knew beyond a shadow of a doubt that God would grant your request the moment you prayed it, what would you pray for at this moment?" My request would be that everyone would have a daily QT with The Living God.

God will speak very personally to you in the QT. I promise (yes, another one). My oldest son used to have the habit of saying, "It's a done deal." I never used that phrase. Some of the words and phraseology of other generations are not even definable to me. I realize that this book has dated me. The chosen hymns alone would do that. They are the ones I grew up with. Each of us will feel more comfortable using the terminology that we grew up with. Future generations will speak new words with new meanings, but The Word of God will not change. And what is more beautifully important is that God will immediately hear and understand all of the new words and phrases that are used in speaking with Him. Each new generation will still use the same three words, "I Love You." God will respond, "I love you too. In fact, I loved you first."

The QT has another nugget of great value. It enhances our trust in our blessed Savior, Jesus Christ. The Cross becomes more real and meaningful. The Cross of Jesus becomes the "T" of Trust.

And I pray that Christ will be more and more at home in your hearts, living within you as you trust in him. May your roots go down deep into the soil of God's marvelous love. (Ephesians 3:17).

Oswald Chambers (*My Utmost For His Highest*, July 6) says that any vision from God must be satisfied at the very highest level. My vision was, "Life is Fragile, Handle With Prayer."

Be Thou my Vision, O Lord of my heart—
Naught be all else to me save that Thou art:
Thou my best thoughts by day or by night—
Waking or sleeping, Thy presence my light.
(Irish hymn translated by Mary E. Byrne, 1880-1931;
See Fettke #382)

As I am ending the hand-written, first draft of this book that God asked me to write, I am being distracted, but I believe Providentially so, by my granddaughter's dog, Elliott. I am dog sitting for a couple of days. Elliott likes me, and after getting over the absence of his mistress, he never leaves my side.

I just looked at him and said to him, "You stick pretty

close don't you?" And he said (some dogs do talk),

"Yes, very close. I always will. "God is like that too.

Good Night, Dear Father.

# WORKS CITED

Babcock, Maltbie D. (1858-1901) and Franklin L. Sheppard (1852-1930). *This is My Fathers World*. (See Fettke #58).

Blackaby, Henry and Norman Blackaby. *Experiencing Prayer with Jesus, The Power Of His Presence and Example*. Sisters, Oregon: Multnomah Publishers, 2006. 45.

Bode, John E. (1816-1874). *O Jesus, I Have Promised*. (See Fettke #369).

Bridges, Matthew (1800-1894). *Crown Him With Many Crowns*. (See Fettke #324).

Byrne, Mare E. (1880-1931). *Be Thou My Vision*. (See Fettke #382).

Carter, Sydney *Lord of the Dance*. 1963.

Chambers, Oswald (1874-1917). *My Utmost For His Highest: an updated edition in today's language: the golden book of Oswald Chambers/edited by James G. Reimann*. Grand Rapids, Michigan: Discovery House Publishers, 1992. Jan. 2, Jan. 17, Jan. 18, Apr. 3, Apr. 18, Apr. 23, May 18, May 22, May 31, June 13, June 19, July 6, July 13, Sept. 9, Sept. 12, Oct. 3.

Deere, Jack. *Surprised By The Power of The Spirit/Surprised by the Voice of God*. Peabody, Massachusetts: Prince Press, 2003.

Fettke. Tom, senior editor. *The Hymnal for Worship & Celebration*. Waco, Texas: Word Music 1986. #51,

#58, #80, #147, #234, #247, #259, #260, #284, #350, #363, #369, #382, #433, #435, #441, #450.

France, Dick. *"The Old Testament in the New Testament"*. Grand Rapids, Michigan: Zondervan Publishing House, 1999. 743.

Graham, Billy. The Way, The Living Bible. Wheaton, Illinois: Tyndale House Publishing, Inc., 1972. 1117.

Hatch, Edwin (1835-1889) and Robert Jackson (1842-1914). *Breathe On Me Breath of God*. (See Fettke #259).

Havergal, Frances (1863-1879) and Robert Schumann (1810-1856). *Lord Speak To Me*. (See Fettke #450).

Henry, Matthew. *Matthew Henry's Commentary on the Whole Bible, Complete and Unabridged*

*In One Volume*, Peabody, Massachusetts: Hendrickson Publisher, Inc. 1991. 1637

Iverson, Daniel. *Spirit of the Living God*. (See Fettke #247).

Johns, Jim and Kaye Johns. *Praying To Make A Difference, A Practical Guide For A Powerful Prayer Life*. Dallas, Texas: The Sampson Company, 1999; (Prayer Power Ministries, Dallas, Texas). 14.

Klein, Laurie. *I Love You, Lord*. House of Mercy/ Maranatha Music, 1978, 1980. (See Fettke #80).

Longstaff, Williams D. (1822-1894) and George C. Steffins (1846-1945). *Take Time To Be Holy*. (See Fettke #441).

Maxwell, John *Partners In Prayer*. Nashville, Tennessee: Thomas Nelson Publishers, Inc., 1996. 14.

Meyer, Joyce. *"Encouraging Everyday Life, Straight From The Heart"*. Fenton, Missouri: Joyce Meyer Ministries, December 2008/January 2009.

Morris, Lelia N., David Read and Kurt Kaiser. *Welcome, Welcome*. Word Music, 1986. (See Fettke #260)

Morton, Timothy S. *"The Greek Game"* – *"A Little Learning Is A Dangerous Thing"*.

Taboo Topics. Sutton, West Virginia: Morton Publications. Web 15, June 2009.

McGee, J. Vernon (1904-1988). *J Vernon McGee On Prayer, Praying and Living In The Father's*

*Will*. Nashville, Tennessee: Thomas Nelson Publishers, 2002. vii, 36, 50.

Osbeck, Kenneth W. *Amazing Grace, 366 Inspiring Hymn Stories for Daily Devotions*. Grand Rapids, Michigan: Kregel Publications, 1990.

Peterson, Eugene. *The Message: The Bible In Contemporary Language*. Colorado Springs, Colorado: NavPress. 2002. 2215.

Prentice, Elizabeth (1818-1878). *More Love To Thee*. (See Fettke #363).

Reynolds, William J., editor. *Baptist Hymnal: We Are Climbing Jacob's Ladder*. Nashville, Tennessee: Convention Press, 1975. #147.

Scriven, Joseph (1819-1886) and Charles C. Converse (1832-1918). *What A Friend We Have In Jesus*. (See Fettke #435)

Sheets, Dutch. Intercessory Prayer, *How God Can Use Your Prayers to Move Heaven and Earth.* Ventura, California: Regal Books, 1996. 82

Scholtes, Peter. *"They'll Know We Are Christians by Our Love".* F.E.L. Publications, 1966. (See Fettke #284).

Smith Eddie. *How To Be Heard in Heaven.* Minneapolis, Minnesota: Bethany House Publishers, 2007. 10-11, 58-59.

Smith, Eddie and Alice Smith. *The Advocates, How to Plead the Case of Others in Prayer.* Lake Mary, Florida: Charisma House, 2001.

Sorge, Bob. *Secrets of the Secret Place, Keys to Igniting Your Personal Time with God.* Greenwood, Missouri: Oasis House, 2006. 28, 119, 194.

Stead, Louisa M. R. (1850-1917) and William J. Kirkpatrick (1838-1921). *'Tis So Sweet to Trust in Jesus*. (See Fettke #350)

Sturch, Sandy. *Bible For The Bewildered and Prayer For The Tongue-Tied, For those who forgot...and those who never knew*. San Antonio, Texas: First Presbyterian Church, 2001.

Swindoll, Charles. *The Hymnal for Worship and Celebration*. Foreword. (See Fettke 1986).

Walford, William (1772-1850) and William Bradbury (1816-1868). *Sweet Hour of Prayer* (See Fettke #433).

Williams, William (1717-1791). *Guide Me, O Thou Great Jehovah*. (See Fettke #51).

Yancey, Philip. *Prayer Does It Make Any Difference*. Grand Rapids, Michigan: Zondervan, 2006.

Young, Ed. *Praying For Keeps*. Nashville, Tennessee:

Serendipity House Publishers, 2004. 4, 78.

# About The Author

From the very beginning, I was totally devoted to this book being authored by The Holy Spirit. The Dedication page sought and recognized authorship – "It's Your Book, Dear Father. Use it as You Will." In Chapter 1, The Heavenly Father was petitioned to "assemble the pieces."

As an instrument of God, I can enumerate some of the God-given, pre-planned talents that He has given. He has given me a capacity to love and to care. He has raised me to love Him although He allowed me to stray. He secured for me a good secular education that included BS, MEd and EdD degrees (Trinity University, San Antonio, Texas and Nova University, Ft. Lauderdale, Florida). He gave me a good linguistic background (talent) that has served me well. He gave me a thirty-five year professional career as a public school teacher, university teacher, and school administrator. He allowed me to write three books to serve school administrators. But most important, He has given me a thirst for the QT that will not be quenched.

As a cooperative author of this book about the QT, I profess no authority or expertise to do so beyond The Holy Spirit enthusing me and drafting the words. I bow to His Glory given to me for His Purpose.

Family-wise, I have three beautiful, successful children all with families of their own, producing eight grandchildren. Fifty three years of marriage oneness is the greatest gift beyond the spiritual intimacy and blessings. Good Morning, Dear Father. I love You.

LaVergne, TN USA
04 March 2010
174946LV00001B/10/P